WHERE THE LIGHT IS

HEIDI E. PATTEE

ISBN: 978-1-7347186-0-7 (full-color paperback edition)
       978-1-7347186-1-4 (b/w paperback edition)
       978-1-7347186-2-1 (eBook edition)

Cover & interior photography by Heidi, Gary, and Isabel Pattee
Author photo by Chad Petska
Cover Design: Redbrush, Lincoln, Nebraska

Woosley-Nash Publishing
Lincoln, Nebraska

Printed in the United States of America by

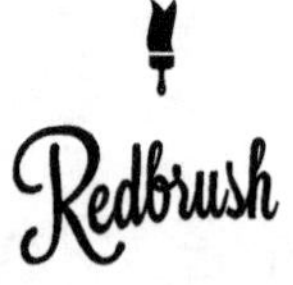

Lincoln, Nebraska

For my husband,
Gary,
and our children,
Nate, Aaron, and Isabel

ACKNOWLEDGMENTS

I am enormously grateful to my husband, Gary, and our three children, Nate, Aaron, and Isabel, for their unending love, encouragement, and support. They not only listened during the creative process, but helped me edit, file for copyright, acquire ISBNs, and navigate computer issues. They are *my light*.

I am also indebted to Lucy Adkins, without whom this book would have stayed hidden among my many papers. It is because of her that I have the added gift of our wonderful Gere Library writing group.

Where the LIGHT Is is a story about the realities of life told through a series of poems.

Sickness, pain, and abuse are all part of our existence, but in the end, loved ones, nature, and art show the prevailing beauty of life.

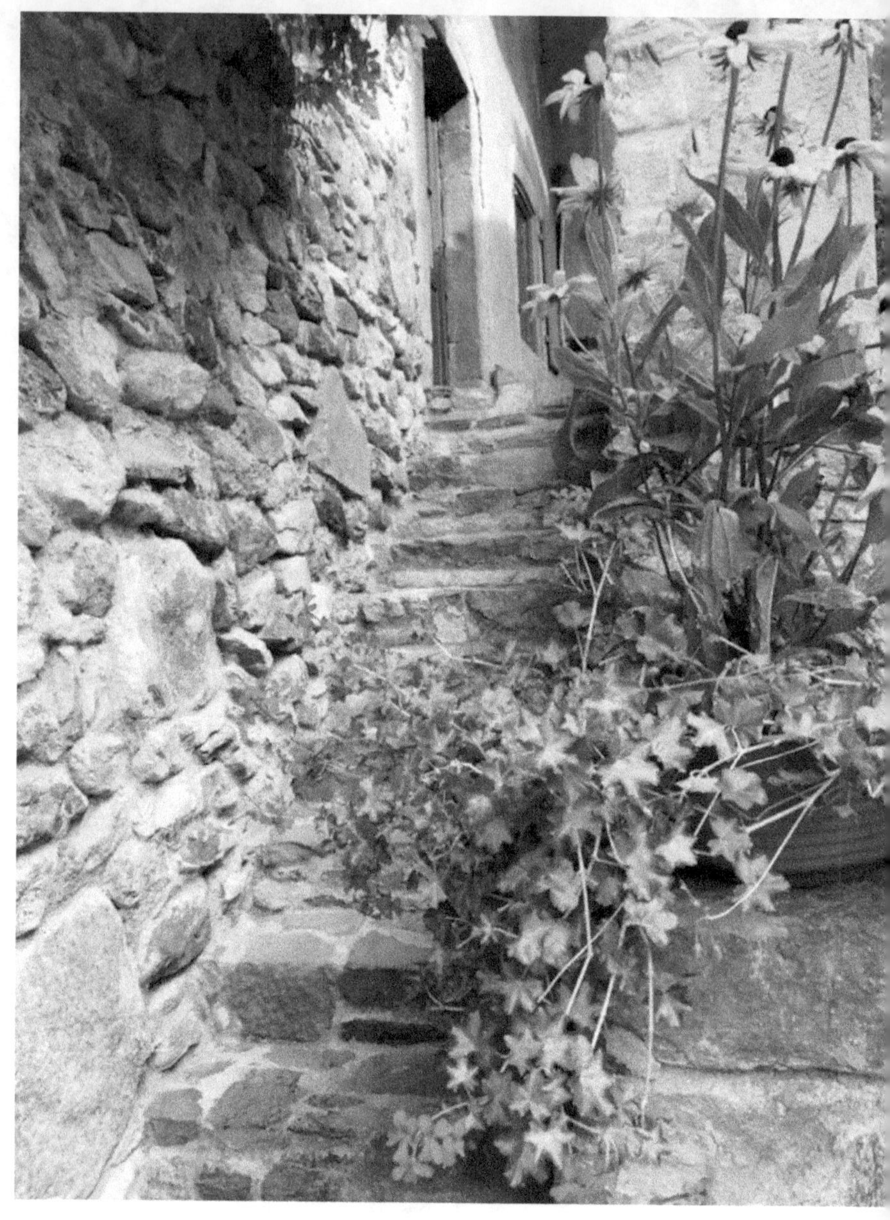

GARY

You pull me out of
Melancholy shallows
That try to
Swallow solace,
You heart
Of my soul,
Now shared.

(1.2019)

NATE

After sixteen hours,
Nate came into the world
Exhausted
From his ordeal,
But beautiful.
And they placed him
Into my arms,
And we knew
Each other.
And I cried,
Because I knew
I would never
Let him feel
Alone.
And I will
Always be there,
Even when
I am no longer.
Because he
Came from me.
Not only from
My flesh,
But from my heart.
And it is a heart
That I will
Always hold.
(III.2018)

AARON

I love to remember
Our trips to the grocery store.
I would place you
In the front of the cart,
Your little legs would dangle,
And you would turn your head shyly
From anyone who looked at you.
You insisted that I stay
Close to you.
When people walked by
In an aisle,
You would reach out
For my neck
With your tiny arms
And pull me down
Towards you.
And we would stay like this as
I would continue to walk,
Bent forward
With your face
Hidden in my neck…
With you feeling secure,
And I feeling
Like I *knew*
What heaven was.
(XI.2018)

OUR DAUGHTER

Is
So responsible.
Calling home
In the fifth grade, no less,
To tell me
That school is out early.
Asking at another time,
"Are you worried?"
This little girl has a
Heart
So big, that she
Leaves an emotional hole
When she is
Not in school,
Not in ballet class.
She is greatly missed
At those times.
I know, because
People always tell me so.
It is true that
Some people are here as
Balm
To other's souls.
(IX.2009)

(for Isabel)

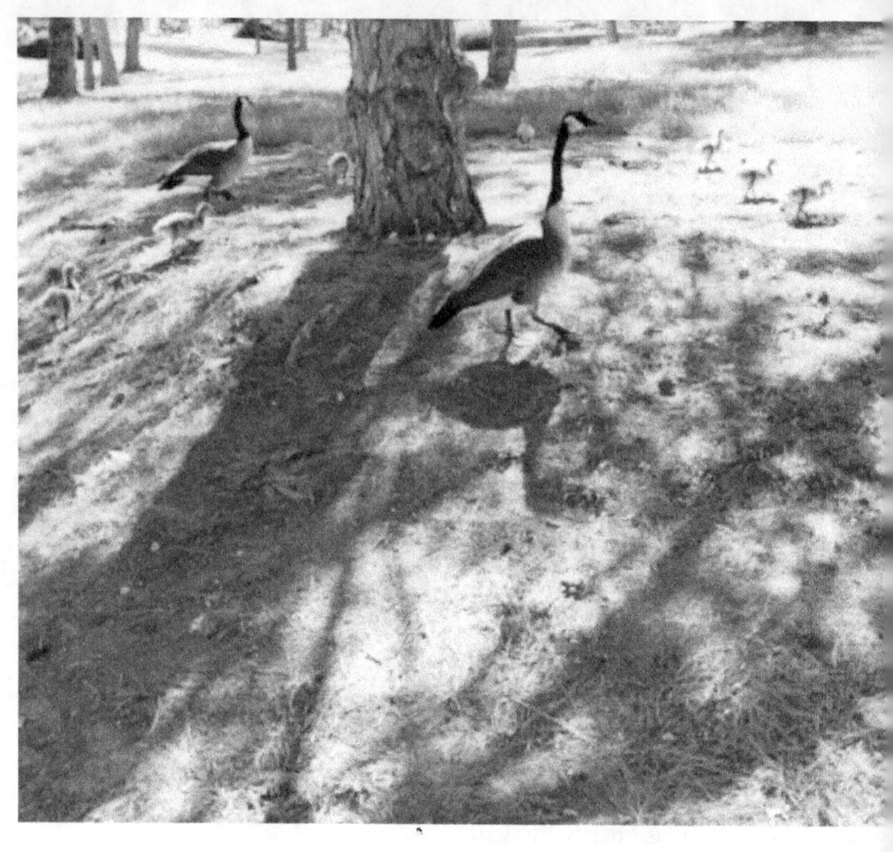

CORD

I saved the little piece left
Of the umbilical cord
That bound
Each child of mine
To me.
I couldn't bring myself to
Throw away that
Last physical bond,
Once my babies began the
Natural process of
Shedding it.
And so I spent a
Lifetime saving
Every tooth,
And carefully
Collecting snippings
From first haircuts,
And more…
Saving every drawing
Ever made
And framing many…
And my children
Know that
That cord,
That once bound us,

Is tied so tightly
Around my heart,
That it could
Never
Be put asunder.

(V.2018)

MY CHILD

You were born
From me,
But I was born
For you.
(IV.2009)

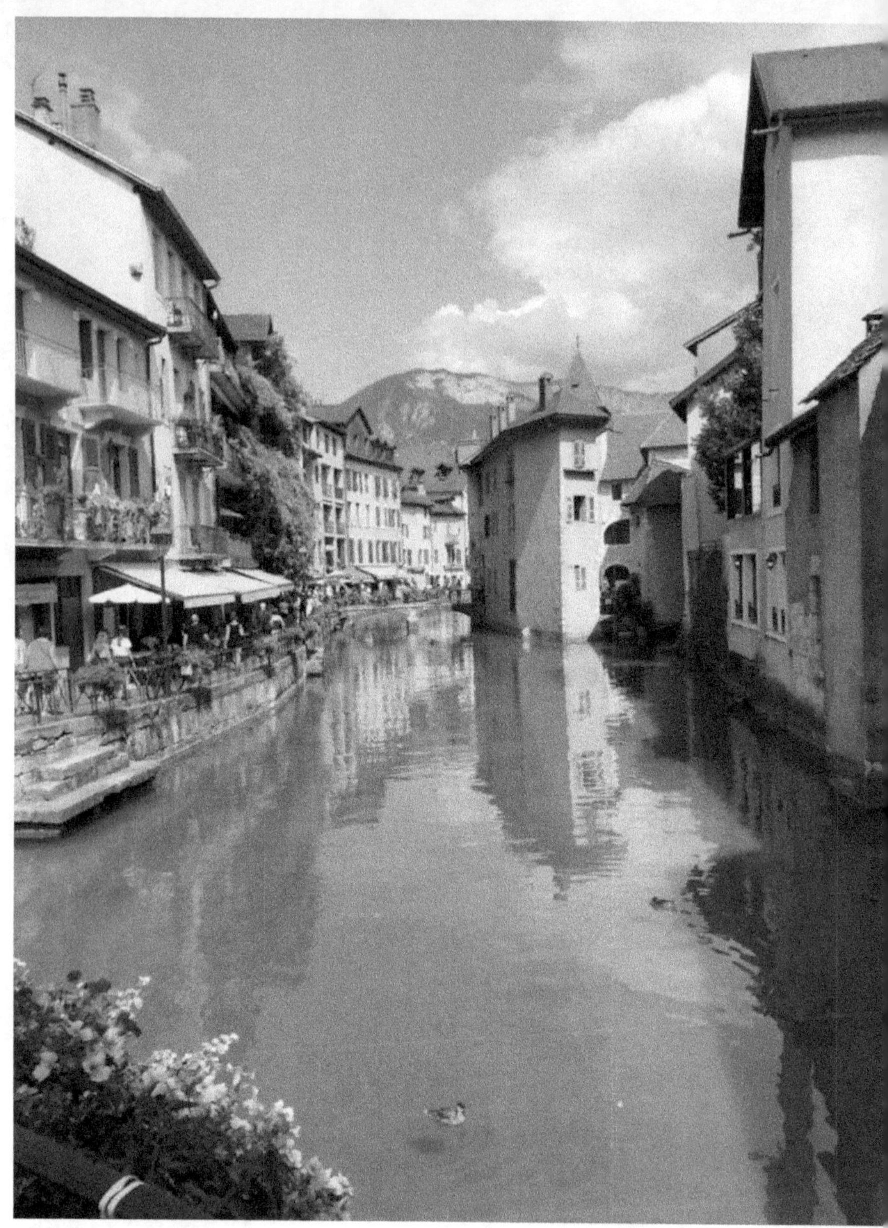

LITTLE THINGS
(WHILE WALKING OUTSIDE)

Sometimes
My heart
Will want to burst
When I see
The young dad kissing
His baby's round little
belly,
Before ever so carefully
Placing his precious
bundle
Into the stroller…
Or the ten-year-old girl,
Standing behind her
father's café chair,
Lovingly rubbing his
almost bald head,
While absentmindedly
gazing over his shoulder
On a lazy summer day…
Little things.
Things that on the
surface
Are so small,
But on the inside,
Are so big.
These
Little things,
These automatic
gestures,
Remind me of when
Our children
Were also these
Little ones,
Doing these
Little things.

(VI.2016)

OUR SONS

I miss

Our sons

Our comedians

Our confidants

Our companions

Our beautiful

Souls

(IX.2009)

OLYMPICS

Watching the Olympics
With our son,
Watching twists and turns
And impossible jumps.
An hour goes by,
Maybe two.
We give our "expert" opinions
About expert athletes.
But then we have to
Say good night
And I love you
And hang up the phone…
To our son,
So very,
Very
Far away.
(11.2010)

WIND

Saturday
Outside in the backyard
On a gliding bench
Wind blowing
Bird chirping
Our dog running back and forth
And back and forth
I'm wondering when the others
Will come home from their bike-ride
Pots brimming with vinca on the deck
On the patio
Where I am sitting
The same wind touching my face
Is gently moving the brush roses
I'm alone on my bench
I'm missing people
The wind reminds me
How our important people
Are like the wind
When they are absent
You will feel them
Breathing about you
You will feel
Their very airy
Embrace
(VI.2010)

GODMOTHER

Beautiful being,

Your fragrant,

Soft soul

Surrounds me.

And I was given your name.

(II.2019)

(for Heidi W.)

OMI

The skin of my
Once smooth face
Is stretched over
Its skull
With a mutt-like
Kind of beauty now.
A beauty derived from the
Jumbled genes of
My multifarious
Ethnic potpourri.
I have a landscape-like face,
Cave-like eye sockets,
Crag-like twin cheeks and
Valley-like wrinkles
That surround my mouth…
Sometimes with fleeting,
Lucky glances in the mirror,
I see my long-gone Omi
Looking back at me,
Living in my face.
(II.2011)

BALLET

I'm not even sure when it all began, this inclination to dance, to be in and with the music. Classical music. Maybe I saw dance on television, I don't know, but my much older grandmother and I would sit in her room, and I would make her tell me all about the theater. About the time in her life when she would go at least once a week and see operas, ballets, plays, or listen to the symphony from her loge. I know she wore ball gowns and kidskin opera gloves, because that was the era. I was told she was beautiful. She was to me. She was sixty-four years older than I, and when she would take me to the city as a child, people still turned to look at her. Maybe it was also at the way she carried herself.

When I was six, she surprised me with tickets to the theater. She hadn't been in decades, not since the death of her son. She said I was ready, that I could behave myself, which meant sitting quietly, and curtsying and bowing my head when meeting people.

I don't remember the name of the piece I saw that night fifty-three years ago. What I did realize was that I knew from that time on exactly what I wanted to do with my life. I wanted to dance. To be in the atmosphere of a stage. To be with *those* people. That's what I knew then.

What I know now is that I have always loved my life with ballet. The acted or the imagined reflecting life. I love the contrast of the light of the stage and the darkness of the house. Most of all, I love the music. Without it I would not move, because it creates the movement within me. I love the training and our melancholy Chopin as we begin pliés at the barre. Because no matter where I am in the world, when my hand wraps around that horizontal piece of wood or metal, I'm at home *in* the music, with *my* people, and surrounded by *our* space.

(11.2019)

ISABEL IN BALLET CLASS

Standing in first position,

One hundred and eighty degrees.

Your neck long.

Your knees tight.

Your arms forming

A crown above your head.

You're an ethereal creature,

Who floats

With arms leading

In beautiful, natural lines

To the music.

Then you see

Your reflection in the mirror,

With mine looking

Back at you…

And you sneak

That *very*

Mischievous smile.

(VI.2010)

SYNESTHESIA

I am not a synesthete,
One of those rare,
Remarkable people,
Who are able,
For instance,
To involuntarily
Pair a certain color
With a particular sound.
But occasionally,
When I see
The colors pink or yellow,
I can hear
The familiar crush
Of light-yellow rosin
Beneath my light-pink
Pointe shoes
In the tiny rosin box.
I can see myself twisting
Each shoe in the sticky
rock-powder
And leaving footprints
On the dance floor
Or stage.
And making sure
That everywhere
I need to make turns

Or land a jump,
There will be rosin,
Protecting me
From a fall
That could
End it all.
(X.2018)

ARABESQUE

Last night,
I was at the barre.
The familiar music
Was in my ears.
It flowed from there
To my foot,
Which slid up my leg
Like a separate animal.
With its
Bony point,
It coursed its way
Behind me
Into a high arabesque.
So high and easy.
So perfect.
Like a dream.
Like a spinal cord injury
Dream.
(l.2011)

SPINAL CORD INJURY

Neck hurts
Hurts all the time
Time to take medicine
Medicine makes me tired
Tired of pain
Pain is part of life
Life that I love
Love that I can walk
Walk and dance
Dance with spinal cord injury
Injuries happen
Happen
(IV.2011)

LITTLE ADAM'S KISSES

Ten-year-old Adam
Wiped the kiss
I gave him
From his cheek
And placed it over
His big heart
With his little hand.
That's what he does
With all of his kisses…
He's had so many,
Since the fall
Onto his head
From two stories
Five years ago.
He's thankful,
Because he can
Walk and talk,
And guide his kisses
Down to his heart.
(X.2010)

ALS (A Love Song)

I can no longer

Hug you,

But I can love the

Hugs from you.

I can no longer speak,

But I can use my eyes

To gaze at you…

To tell you

That I will forever

Love you.

(XI.2017)

RED TULIPS

I am a card and letter writer
And today I received
A thank you card.
A thank you card
For a birthday card.
It read,
"The card with the picture of
Red tulips
Reminded me of the bouquets
I would receive every birthday
From my mother.
It's been seventeen years,
Since my last
Red tulips."

(11.2011)

(for Goti)

HAIKU-*THOUGHT*

It suddenly comes.

This bombarding thought of mine.

My pencil takes it.

(X.2017)

HAIKU-*LEAD*

You beautiful lead!
Soft flowing blackness coming.
My faithful pencil.

(X.2017)

WILLIAM KLOEFKORN

Your radio show,
"Poetry of the Plains",
Was a weekly ritual
I looked forward to
When I was in my car alone.
The soothing tenor of your voice
Kept me company.
You painted verbal masterpieces which
Kept me entranced
For a few moments in time.
You made me see spoken images by
Creating word pictures.
And so my car
Became your museum
Until a little after three,
When the final school bell rang and
My children climbed in.
(V.2009)

SCHOOL BUS

I liked riding the three-thirty bus home
from school.

It was a peaceful time.

There were no teachers giving assignments.

It was also a noisy time,

With the excited chatter of friends

Finally getting to talk.

I used to like looking out of the window

At the tranquil German villages

As I was being brought home…

The road leading from school

To my village

Had only two lanes,

But was busy.

Busy with traffic.

Busy with trafficking.

Busy with women-of-the-night,

Who could take their places

No earlier than three pm…

Each day

I watched quietly

From my bus window as

The Americans,

The Germans, and

The French,

Conducted post-war

International Trade.

(V.2018)

PURSE

In the fourth grade
I met Tina.
We were alike,
In that we were
Both German
And so, we didn't fit into
The American school.
Our clothes were different.
Our mothers had accents.
The occasional kid called us Nazis.
But Tina
And her three minions
Bullied me
Until the eighth grade,
When she was
Kicked out of school.
So I went
To the place in the attic
Where I found the
Belongings of my mother's
Dead brother.
And I began to carry a purse
Like the other girls.
And the purse contained
A pocket knife and
My uncle's brass knuckles.
(XI.2017)

ANTON'S GIFT

I see Anton in my mind.

I am a child again, maybe nine, and he is a five-year-old in a thirty-something body, wearing a shabby three-piece suit, and a three-day-old beard.

He stops at our front wrought-iron gate and calls for my mother to come out; they grew up together in our village.

She, though, is hurriedly trying to get our evening meal prepared, so she tells me to go outside, give him a piece of fruit, and talk to him for a while.

I do, but he asks where *she is*.

So I tell him she's cooking, that she can't come out every time, and I give him the fruit.

He takes it, pleased to be receiving it from me again.

Then his face lights up as he reaches into his left suit jacket pocket.

He says he has a gift for me that he has found on the ground in the forest, and in his hand is cupped the most delicate, small, dead bird.

I look at the beautiful creature with its opalescent eyes, tiny, fragile feet, and slightly iridescent feathers, and I know that he is giving me what he treasures most.

This is what he always does, so I thank him and tell him that I can't accept it.

Anton smiles shyly at me, relieved, as he carefully places his bird back into its pocket-nest that he has made for it.

He turns to leave and I tell him good-bye until next time, when I know Anton will offer me another dead animal and I will give him another piece of fruit.

(1.2018)

(in memory of the real "Anton")

VETERAN

Silke was in the kitchen and glanced out of the window, while standing at the sink doing dishes.

The familiar man with his walking stick and cigar caught her glance as he passed the gate on his way to the forest.

He smiled and nodded with that little bow of the head that always gave away men of his generation.

She didn't really know him, but in a way, still grew up with him.

After the dishes, ten-year-old Silke and her brother went outside and headed for the edge of the forest, where their best friends lived.

Three brothers, who made her secretly wish she were also a boy.

As the five of them started out, the man passed them, this time with the other side of his body to them.

The side from which he had no face, but his smile still shone.

(XI.2017)

FAMILIAR VOICE

I spoke with my
Teenage best friend
Yesterday,
After too many years of
Yesterdays.
Her familiar voice
Brought back
The comfort
Of someone
Who knows me well.
And time,
And distance,
Seem not
To have
Diminished us.
(VIII.2010)

FRIENDS

Through distance,
And seasons,
Time has faded
Memories of
Cities visited at eighteen.
Heavy backpacks.
Reading books on trains.
Laughing together about
Things only we knew.
Walking with linked arms
And long hair.
The apartment in Paris…
The horse in the park in Madrid…
But mainly,
I remember the laughing:
Rippling,
Unstoppable,
Infectious…
(IX.2009)

TWO GIRLS ON TRAINS

We travelled through the

Ancient

Cities of

Germany,

France,

Spain,

Italy, and

Switzerland.

But during our

Backpacking escapade,

When we sat

On the trains,

We read.

And I read of the formation of the

Ancient

North American Continent.

And so I was

At eighteen,

Two places

At once.

(1.2018)

WOMAN IN A BLUE DRESS

Isabel and I waited with our luggage
Near the door of the train car.
The small area was crammed with people of
all sorts;
Hot, sweaty, and some stinking.
Not far from us stood a woman
In an electric blue dress that landed just a little
above the knee.
She had her hair pulled back neatly into a bun,
Wore mirrored aviator sunglasses,
And matching long silk-thread earrings.
I turned my head over to her slowly
With a kind of bored waiting-look,
When the woman reached up her hand
And began to distractedly
Pick her nose.

(VII.2018)

ROOTS

I want to go home
Stop the back and forth
Complete the circle
Feel my roots again
I am a tree
Without a forest

(II.2010)

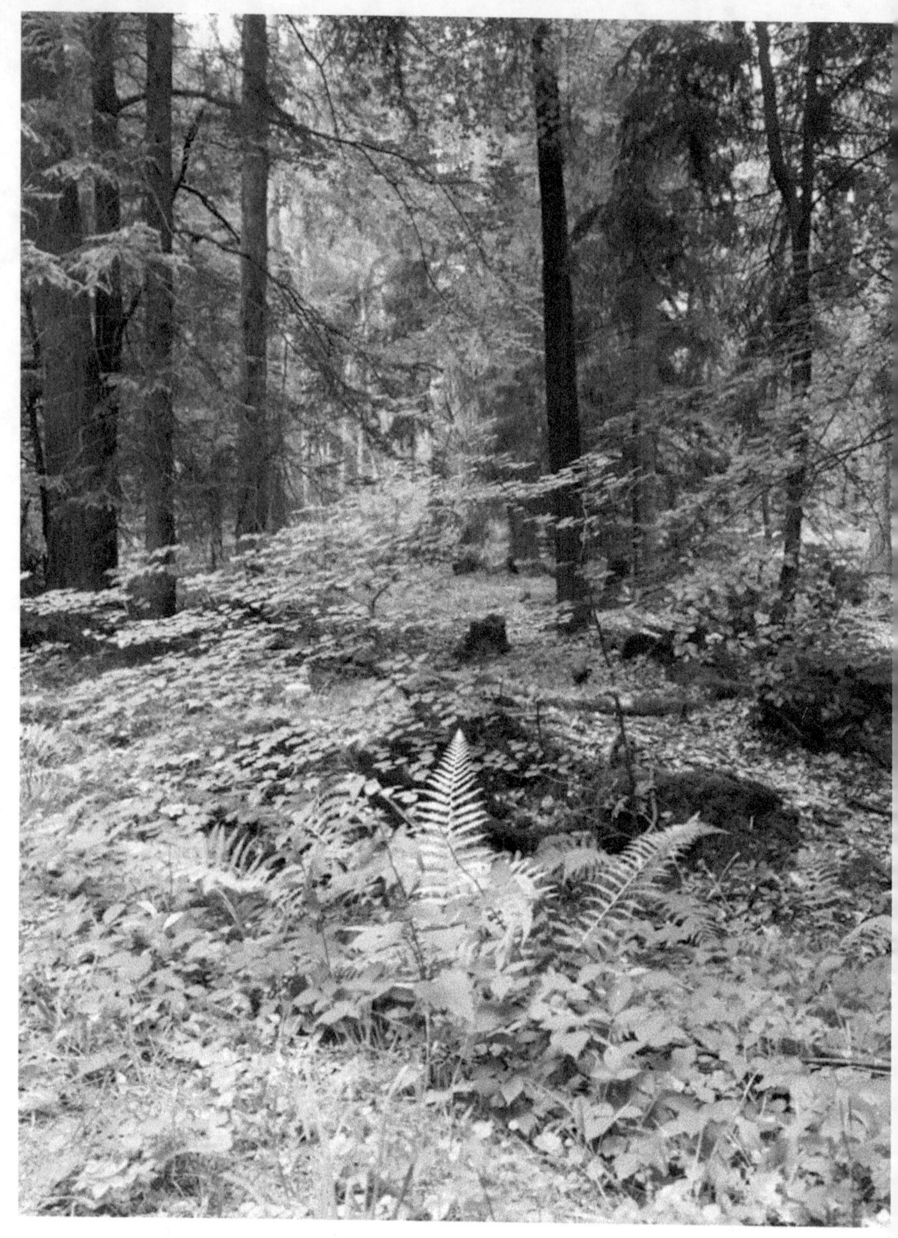

A LETTER TO MY FOREST

Tell me

if you miss the dark silence of the mature,
soaring, aromatic fir trees.

Tell me

if you miss the way they stood as sentinels.
Strong and elegant in their green uniforms,
allowing me to pass among their quiet ranks.

Tell me

if your heart mourns as mine, that the
windstorm destroyed the noble army that
protected me. That gave me solace.

(III.2018)

TREE

In the forest was a Tree.

A Tree that was different from the others.

It was larger, with long branches that
reached out like arms.

And it was loved by a seven-year-old girl, who
would grab her doll and run alone from her home

into the forest to her Tree.

Her mother had shown her the path and had
told her to run when she heard the sirens.

And so she did.

Over, and over, and over again.

Until one day, the sirens stopped sounding.

And the bombs stopped dropping…

The girl grew up and old, but never stopped
going to her Tree.

And after many storms, and after too many wars,
her Tree began to die and fall.

And the once little girl visited the once great
trunk, and the once great branches now lying on
the ground.

And her grief was overwhelming.

(VI.2018)

(for my Mother)

SINCE YOU SAW HER LAST

Since you saw her last
You have not spoken.
You have not spoken,
Because she has not called,
Because she must
Be the one who always calls
Her parents.
It's how it has always been.
How it has been until now.
When you broke
The last little
Piece
Of her heart.

(XI.2017)

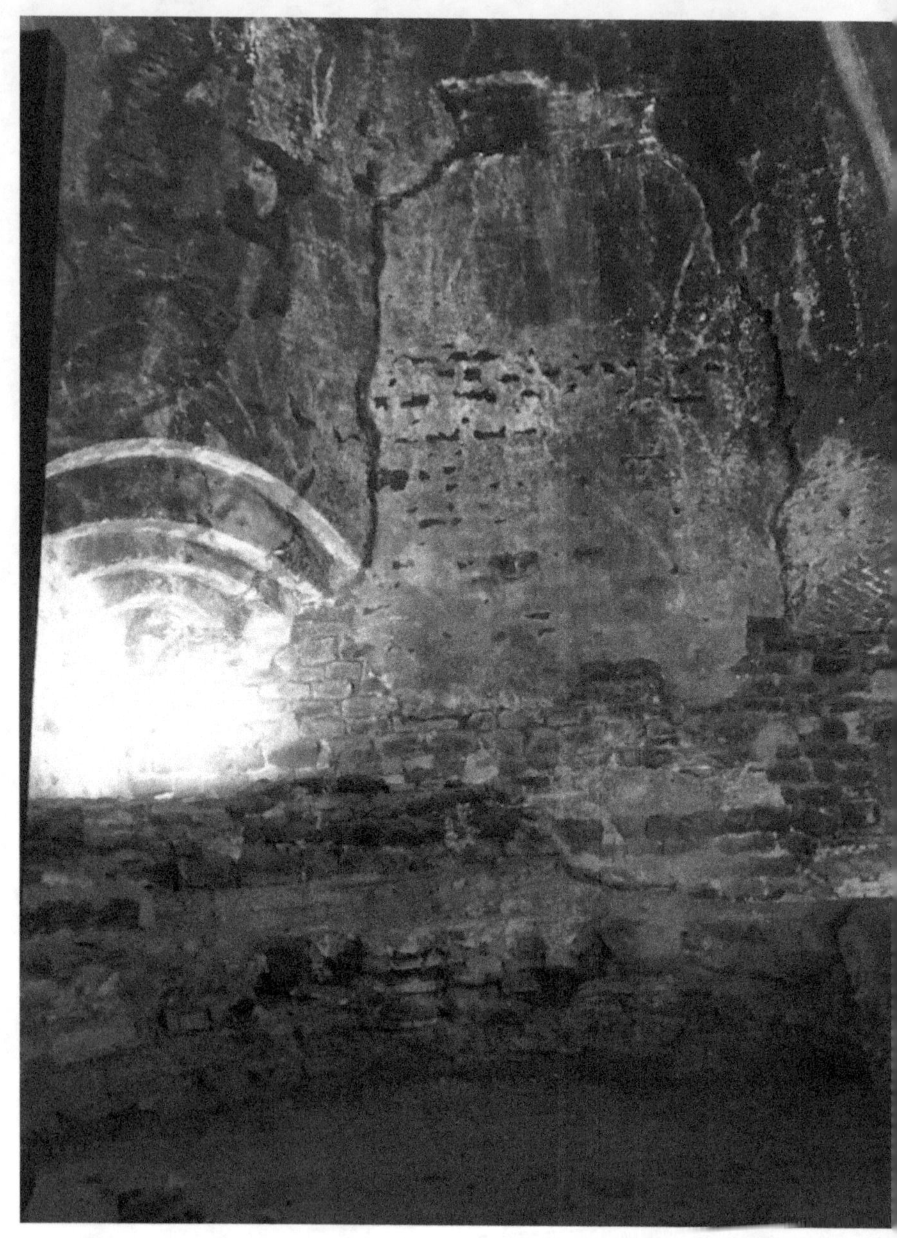

SILVER

She has learned
To let go
Of the things
Her parents have said.
Of the things
Her parents have done.
And hold on instead to
The good things.
Even though
Those good things
Have become like silver,
So badly tarnished,
The metal is almost
Unrecognizable.
And after every phone call,
She cleans and
She polishes,
So that she doesn't
Allow her soul
To darken.

(III.2018)

BLUE-GREEN

Pulled by her rib-long hair up the curved
staircase, up to her little room.

Pulled by her right arm, while a two-inch belt
cracks down on her naked back, thighs, and
underwear-only-clad bottom.

She's sixteen.

Punishment for a bad grade in French.

Her father is with the belt.

Her mother with the hair.

Sometimes they do work together well.

She doesn't remember anymore what happened
when she got to her room…

When they left and went downstairs again…

The next day, or so, her sister and she, as
usual, share the bathwater.

As she sheds her clothes, her sister looks at her
body, at the long blue-green, two-inch welts
that weave their way across the back of her
torso and thighs.

And her sister cries silently into the bathwater.

(VIII.2017)

DREAM TWO DAYS BEFORE MOTHER'S DAY

I dreamed
That my mother
Laid the fresh-cut herbs
from the garden
Onto the dining room
table,
Instead of in the kitchen.
That was odd,
Because normally,
China plates and sterling
silver
Would be set there.
In my dream,
I asked my mother
If I could help her.
But she said
No,
And that she would
prepare everything
Herself.
So I waited a short while
Before I went into the
kitchen
To offer again.

And when I did,
I found
The others there.
Helping.
And my mother
Turned,
Looked at me,
And smiled.
That smile.

(V.2018)

INGE

Our neighbor-lady
Was kind to us as children,
And then to our children.
She always seemed
So very tall.
So very imposing.
But she understood us.
And loved us.
So we went to her.
Because she *knew*.
Even though we
Never really *told* her everything…
Then one day,
We heard she died in her living room.
Quietly.
Modestly.
Just like she lived.
But her memory is
Not quiet or modest.
It lives on in us.
So very tall.
So very imposing.
(VII.2009)

KNIVES

Over her desk is a perpetual calendar.

It records the birthdays and events of significant people in her life.

It's the New Year, so she flips the calendar page from December to January…

She sees it's their birthdays again.

Her parents' birthdays.

Only this year it's different.

They're alive, but she's dead.

To them.

Again.

The first time was when she was twenty-two.

She's fifty-nine now.

They don't want to hear the sound of her voice.

When she looks at January tenth and twentieth, she wonders how a calendar manages to turn Numbers into Knives.

(1.2019)

VOID

The

Void

His father left in his heart was a gaping, expanding

Hole.

But by the time his own three children were grown,

He realized he had carefully stitched the

Hole

With threads of security and sanctuary.

And the devastating

Void

His father created, had become only the tiniest

Hole

In his

Soul.

(1.2012)

(for Gary)

D.C. KOREAN WAR MEMORIAL

I see now, what you must have looked like, Daddy.

Young, with a gun, eyes on the look-out.

Knowing tomorrow was only a Maybe, and
that Death was eagerly awaiting you with each
new step.

That same Death you defied as a milk-faced
WWII soldier.

I see the rain poncho covering a heavy backpack.

The fatigue in your face.

The near brokenness.

I can only imagine the loss you feel, because you
will tell only the funny stories.

The buddy stories.

For this is how you've learned to live with your
memories…

And leave them in the shadows of your mind.

(XI.2009)

ALARM

It's peaceful
And I'm in the backyard
With my eleven-year-old daughter
On the bench-swing,
Listening to her school story…
A car alarm goes off,
Which sounds like
A siren…
And I'm reminded of
What I read this morning…
That in Iraq,
A bomb
Has killed
Another mother's
Child today.

(VIII.2010)

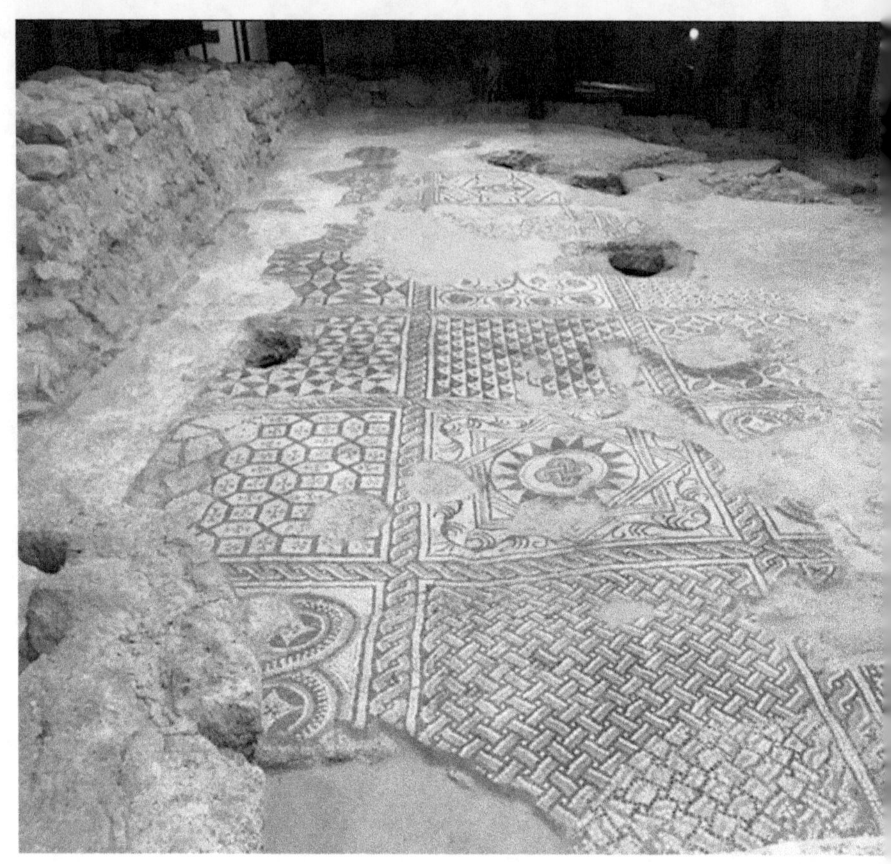

MOSAIC

I imagine our children
Around the table
Laughing,
Stuffing themselves with stuffing.
Someone asking for gravy.
Again.
Even though
I've made a lot,
And even placed a portion
Of the liquidy-brown ambrosia
On each end
Of our festive spread.
Thanksgiving at our home
Is happy.
Unbroken.
Shaped by the two of us,
Who grew up a little
Broken.
But we took our
Broken little pieces
And created
Our beautiful
Mosaic.
Our beautiful,
Laughing,
Gravy-eating
Mosaic.
(XI.2018)

THE POT

The little pot
In the kitchen
Used to be enough,
Until our children began
Bringing home their friends.
And so, I bought
A big pot.
Because I had to
Always
Have enough
For when one of our children
Called and asked,
"Can Matt eat with us tonight?"
And so it happened that
Evan, Kali, Chris, Xing, Ben,
Adam, Cole, Ashley,
And many more,
Were the beloved friends,
Who ate with us…
And sometimes
Even lived with us…
And so
Our big pot
Became our bountiful,
Beautiful
Melting Pot.
(XII.2018)

LUNGS

Drinking coffee
In the kitchen,
The clock is
Ticking rhythmically.
The windows are closed,
But I hear
The faint sound
Of cars with revved-up mufflers
Speeding down the street.
The air is already heavy
And hot outside,
And I struggle
To breathe…
But in this semi-solitude
I hear
Lungs.
A rhythmic
Letting in-and-out of air.
Much like
The slow breaths of
Our faithful Max,
Curled up on his
Long-gone dog mat
Near the table…
But appliances can
Fool you that way.
(IX.2017)

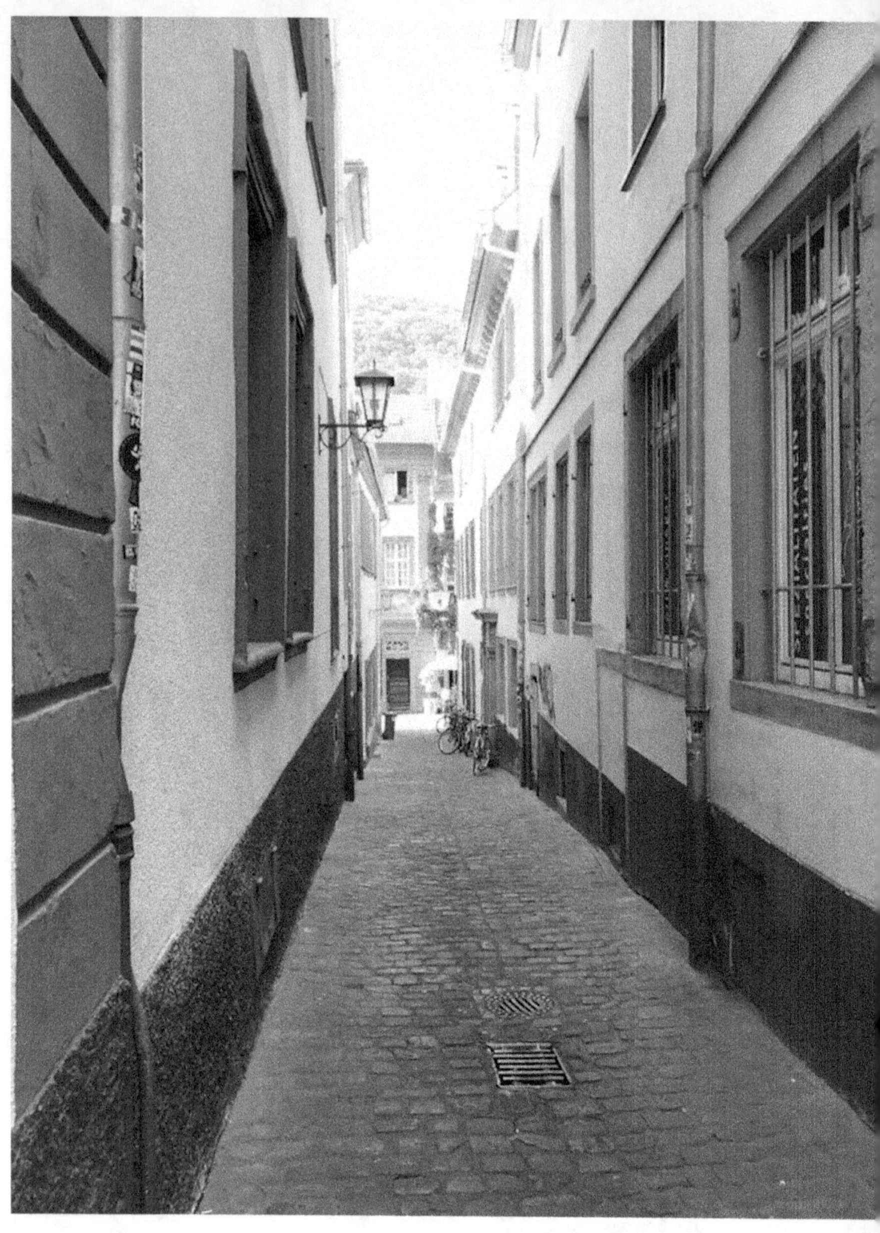

DOOR

I have a dream about
My house,
About two extra rooms
On the second floor
That I rarely go into.
They are rooms with
Furniture and objects
I didn't buy,
Wasn't given.
I don't know why the
Rooms are there,
And why
When I wake,
They disappear.
In my real house,
I lock and alarm my
doors.
But in my dreams
The house has this
Door,
That has an ancient
Bolt,
That has trouble locking,
That leads to
A sidewalk.
And strangely,
There is a table with a
Large, but low green
plant
And two smaller ones.
They have recently been
Watered.
But by whom?
And I realize that
Anyone could have
Entered my home
Through this door
At any time.
Because it was
On a city sidewalk.
But no one did.
And why was I
Kept safe?

(IX.2017)

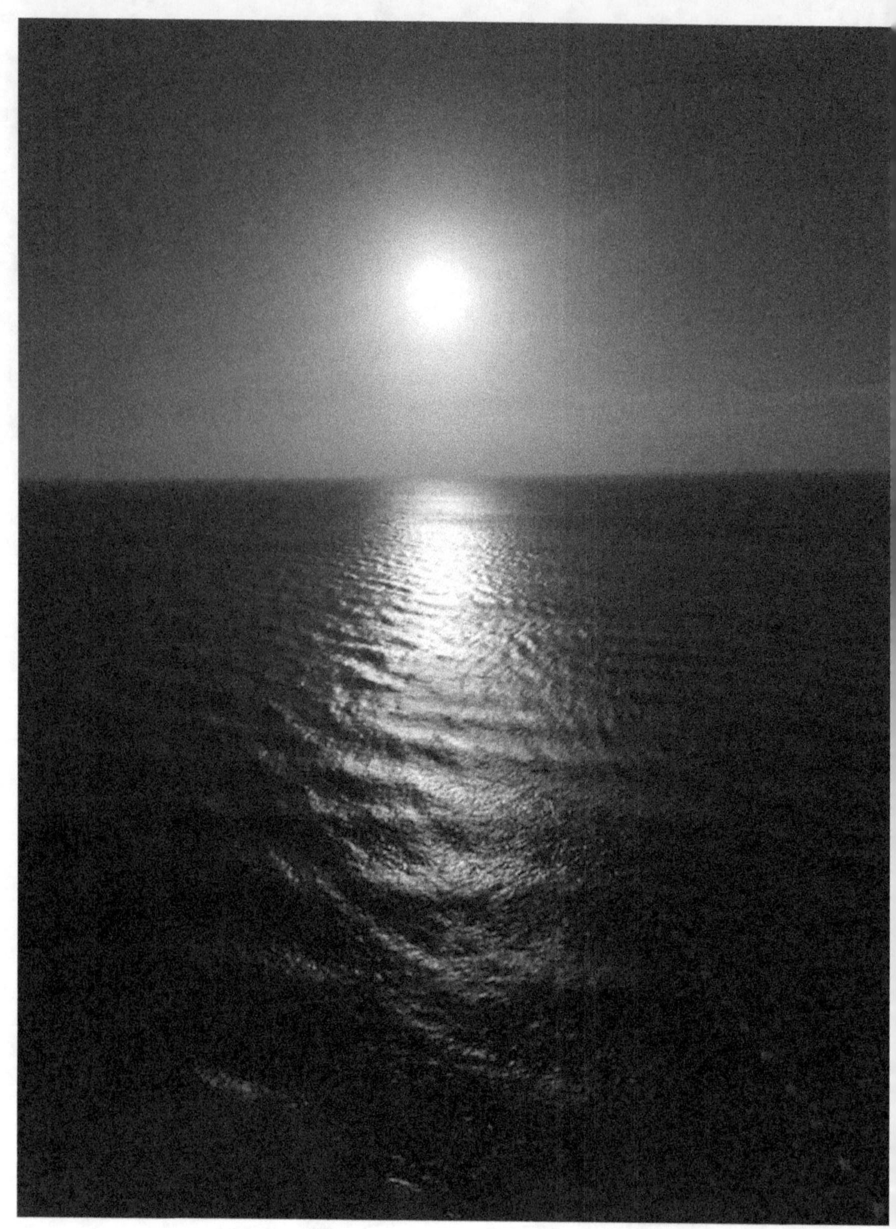

SWIMMING

Swimming
In the ocean
Where it's deep and
Getting deeper.
Her arms are tired.
So are her legs.
Her long hair sways behind her head
In graceful swirls
And it's all that can be seen.
But the thoughts from that head
Ever so carefully,
Ever so slowly,
Carry her safely
Onto the shore.
(1.2019)

OLD FILM

They were Young
And naïve,
When their Old
Uncle did
What he did,
With his voice,
With his hands,
With his body.
And for
Decades,
They wished him
Dead.
The sisters.
Because the scenes
Haunted their heads,
Like reels of
Old film,
And they wanted
It gone.
And finally,
He *was* gone.
But not the
Old film.
The decades
Old film.
(11.2019)
(for C&H)

NOW

You're going to jail,
You family friend.
You uncle.
You touched a six-year-old.
You touched her sister.
Now You say
You touched "inappropriately".
Well,
The police have
You Now.
Have arrested
You Now,
Because after
Ten years,
Their father
Now knows.
Now You
Will enter
Your prison,
So they can
Begin
To leave theirs.
(X.2010)
(newspaper)

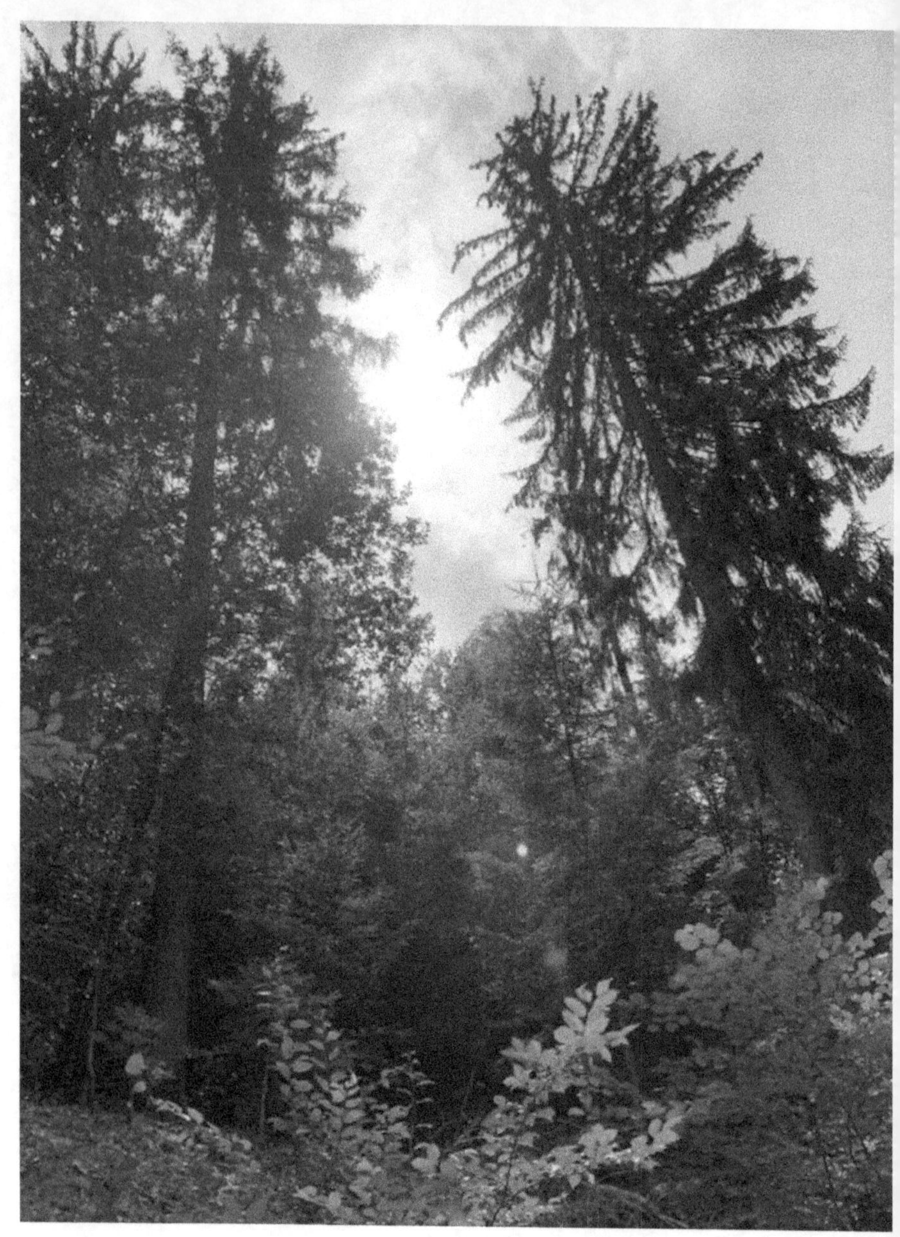

LIGHT IN THE HOURGLASS

Dark
Memories
Run heavy in time through
The *ruminating* hourglass;
Its sand fills bags in the mind,
Creating a disconsolate
Darkness…

Until
Brightness
Pierces the bags.
And then that weighty sand begins
To run out and away,
So that what is left is
Light
In the hourglass.
(III.2019)

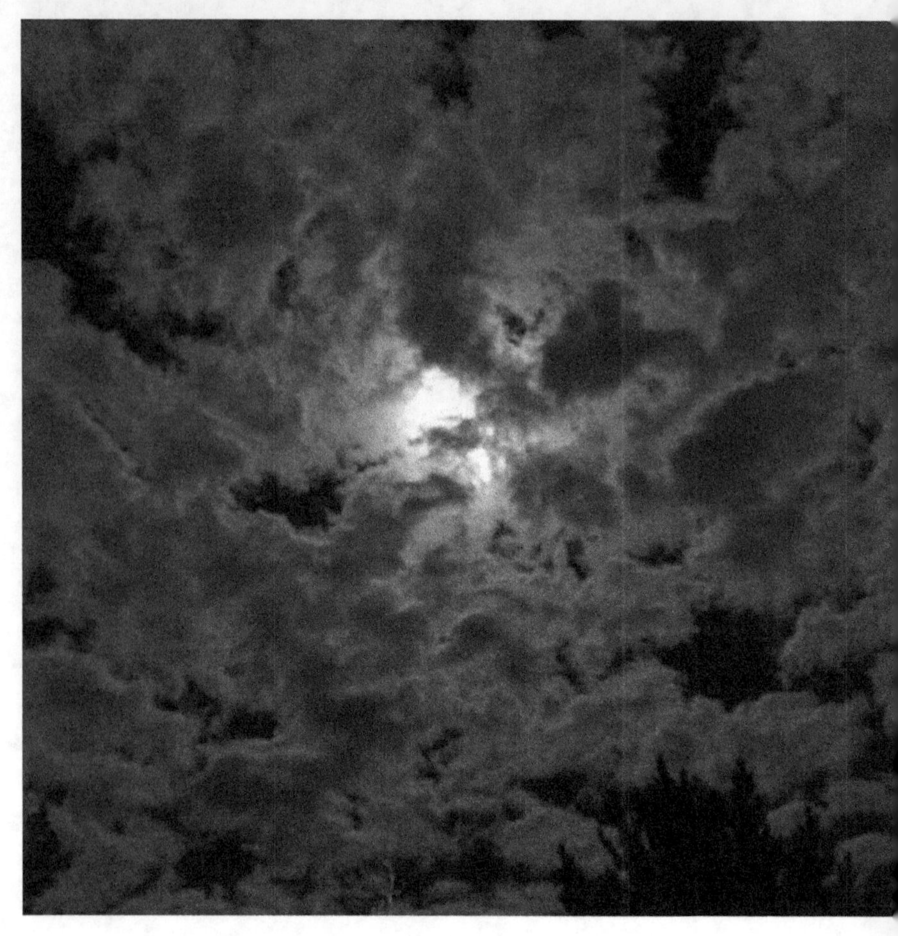

NIGHT

Darkness
Of the night surrounds me
But its moon envelopes me
With an ethereal blanket
Of soft filtered
Light

(1.2013)

FOR MY COMPANION ON FATHER'S DAY

"Never have a companion who casts you in
the shade",
Wrote the seventeenth century Jesuit
philosopher, Baltasar Gracián.
Since it is a human yearning to be valued,
What are the attributes of the companion
who values?
Perhaps honor, humility, and incorruptibility
would be a few descriptors of such an individual,
Since he would be one who feels confident
in his own being.
There is therefore little need for self-
aggrandizement and self-absorption.
He is content, because his life is consumed in a
mission, with ambition,
Not merely wishing or wasting.
So what is the effect of those attributes on the
companion's companion?
Similarly, how does the companion's behavior
Affect the family and further furrow into the
world surrounding them?

The simple act of one individual not
placing another,
Whom he is close to "in his shade",
Affects not merely the one whom he has
not shaded.

The unshaded is accorded light, honor, and respect,
And this light radiates onto their children.
Since the children see these principles enacted,
They emerge from this union as members
of society,
Who will conceivably do the same.
Who will not fall into egoism, arrogance,
and vainglory.
So what does it mean to have this kind of
companion?
It means that no matter what life's trials are,
He will venture to keep you unshaded.
And that in your darkest hours,
You may be assured that he
Is a source of light,
Not darkness.

(IV.2019)

(for Gary)

ICARUS

Flying high
In the sky
Above the ocean,
We, in the great
Belly of our bird,
Turn,
And like
Icarus,
Threaten to
Fly too near
To the sun.
(VIII.2018)

IN FLIGHT

High above the ground,
Yet just below the clouds,
Are snow covered
Farm fields
Resembling
Peaceful,
Newly raked,
Zen gardens…

Then overhead,
The crackling,
Cacophonous voice
Of the flight attendant
Is heard.

(11.2010)

COTTONWOOD-DOWN IN THE SPRINGTIME

Swirling

Twirling

Whirling

Downy cottonwood seeds

Fill the air

I go out

And join their

Delirious dance

Ethereal white

Bright

Floating

Flowing

Feather-like bodies

A natural

Swan Lake

Surrounds me

(IV.2010)

LEOŠ JANÁCEK

Once
While listening to your music
So sublime
I saw nothing but a
Black
Stage
With stark
Flitting dancers
In minimalist
White
Costumes
And I managed
To pull over
In my car
To avoid
A collision
(VIII.2009)

HAITI

Cradle of poverty,

Anguish.

Cradle of music,

Bright art.

Cradle which rocked.

Earthquake which knocked

At each door,

Sparing few…

A new

Generation of amputees,

Who still dance

To the drumbeat

Of their hearts.

(1.2010)

MUSIC

Elation

Because someone is playing with the
accomplishment of Liszt

Joy is

Transcendent

(11.2014)

ROSES OF SHARON

Our Roses of Sharon
Are flooded with
Blossoms
Of pink and purple
More than you can count
And above these
Blossoms
Are hundreds of
Butterflies
Of gold and amber
Gently landing
Bejeweling
Sharon

(IX.2017)

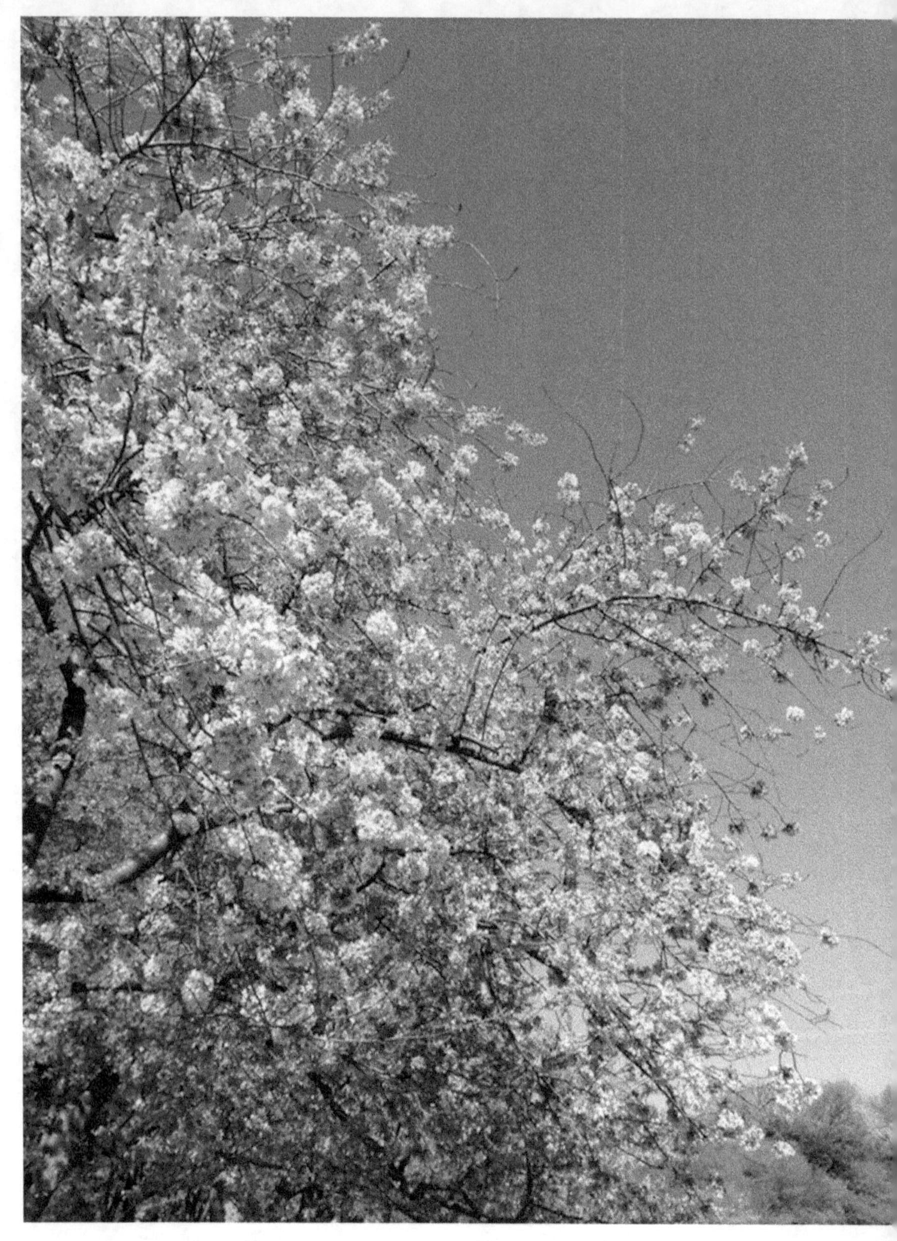

SPRING

Fragile Buds
Are coming out of brown sticks,
Which are hiding the
Life that is coursing through them.
Soon we will see
Little Leaves,
Carefully unfolding themselves
Into heart-shaped escorts,
Waiting for their dates. The
Delicate Flowers,
Meanwhile, are slowly growing,
Beginning to show
What will eventually become
Gossamer Petals…
Those beautiful evening gowns
Of various colors,
At once charming,
Wondrous,
Fragrant.
And up next to them,
Like tender lovers,
The now fully
Grown Leaves.
(IV.2011)